Breaking Up With the Cobalt Blues

Poems for Healing

Lindsay Soberano Wilson

Breaking up With the Cobalt Blues: Poems for Healing
Author: Lindsay Soberano Wilson

lindsaysoberano@gmail.com

ISBN 978-1-962374-25-5 Paperback

ISBN 978-1-962374-26-2 EBook

Library of Congress Control Number: 2024913186

Published by Prolific Pulse Press LLC
ProlificPulse.com

Contact: admin@prolificpulse.com

Published in Raleigh North Carolina USA
Paperback Publication Date: August 2024

Review

Poetry can serve all the purposes for the reader and writer. For the writer, Lindsay, it's a method to document the past and learn from it...to be empowered by it. Lindsay's poems in her epic collection Breaking Up With the Cobalt Blues purge and process the difficulties of her experiences into quantifiable outbursts of creative prose. She is an artist on a mission, using her gifts and traumas to offer many pages of healing. For the reader, healing opportunities are abundant through offered blessings and, perhaps, through seeing familiar patterns and events from their own lives - a light shown on them to provide the context that may have alluded them, finally revealed to offer the beginnings of a path forward. Read these poems to discover a glimpse into your own pain. Read them for their glimpse of encouragement and support. Read them because maybe they'll show you how art can make you whole. It's certainly cheaper than therapy...and no doubt, more enjoyable too.

Rick Lupert,
Author of It's Spritz O'Clock Somewhere and God Wrestler: a Poem for Every Torah Portion /
RickLupert.com

This book contains sensitive subject matter that may be distressing to some readers. Please take care of yourself and prioritize your well-being while reading. If you find the content overwhelming, consider taking a break or seeking support from a trusted individual or mental health professional.

Table of Contents

Dedication

Dedicated to my guardian angels
~ only the good die young ~
brave hearts
James Buchanan (1975-2017)
and
Dylan Shulman(1977-2003)
Rest In Peace, Always and Forever.

Acknowledgements

"A Hummingbird Sang To Me Today" *Scribe*
"A Love Letter to Montreal" *Put It To Rest*
"A New Day" *iPoetry*
"Above the Watermark" *Fine Lines Journal 32.1*
"Are You Sure?" *iPoetry*
"Black Light Dragonfly" *iPoetry*
"Black Swan Song" *iPoetry*
"Bleeding Hearts" *Put It To Rest*
"Blindsided" *iPoetry*
"Blood Orange Heart" *iPoetry; Fevers of the Mind*
"Blue Moon Heart" *iPoetry*
"Bluebells" *iPoetry*
"Bounce and Flow are Gifted" *Scribe*
"Breaking Up With The Cobalt Blues" *Scribe*
"I - Butterflies in My Belly" *Put It To Rest*
"II - Butterflies In Their Bellies" *Put It To Rest*
"Butterfly Lady" *Put It To Rest*
"I - Carving Space For You" *Scribe*
"Catch Up to my Feelings" *Put It To Rest*
"Chasing Demons" *iPoetry*
"Closer to Truth" *Put It To Rest*
"Come Undone" *Put It To Rest, Fevers of the Mind*
"Cruising" *Put It To Rest*
"Dancing Through the Dark" *iPoetry; Cadence*
"Even When I'm Careful" *Put It To Rest*
"Every Rose Has A Thorn" *iPoetry, Fevers of the Mind*
"Find Something You Love" *Put It To Rest; Cadence*
"Finding Rest in the Unrest of a Friend's Suicide" *Put It To Rest*
"First Choice" *Fine Lines Journal 32.1*
"Flickering Lights" *iPoetry*
"Fluorescent Lights" *iPoetry*

"For Shame" *iPoetry*
"Fortress" *Athanasy: The Inner World Anthology*
"Get Our Hands Dirty" *Put It To Rest*
"Give and Take" *iPoetry*
"Glimmers" *iPoetry*; *Cadence* (Prolific Pulse Press), *Musical Composition by Dr. Ken Metz*
"Grief" *Put It To Rest*
"He Saved My Life, But He Died Young, So I Pay It Forward" *Put It To Rest*
"Hope, Are You There?" *Embrace of Dawn*
"How I Became a Poet" *Put It To Rest*
"How to Live" *Put It To Rest*
"Hurt So Good" *iPoetry*
"I Call This Trauma" *Poetry Pause; Fresh Voices Issue 22, Put It To Rest*
"I Played Dead" *Put It To Rest*
"I Used to Look Away" *iPoetry*
"I Waited For You" *Scribe*
"I Will Remember" *Put It To Rest*
"I Tripped on a Wound Today" *Scrittura*
"In the Pure and Bloody Waters" *iPoetry*
"Into the Woods" *iPoetry*
"It Doesn't Make You Ugly" *Put It To Rest*
"It Was Never A Big Deal" *Put It To Rest*
"It's A Love-Hate Thing" *Put It To Rest*
"I've Climbed Mountains" *iPoetry, Spillwords Press*
"Just Out of Touch" *iPoetry*
"Know Your Worth" *Put It To Rest*
"Let It Pass Through You" *Put it To Rest*
"Let My Hurt Go" *Put It To Rest*
"Like a Fault Line" *Put It To Rest*
"Like A Glitzy Dress on a Hanger" *Put It To Rest*
"Like A Muse In A Cage" *Marlene in a Pub; Fevers of the Mind, Avalanches in Poetry*

"like a paper cut" *Poetry Pause, Put It To Rest*
"Like An Iceberg" *Put It To Rest*
"Like Rapaccini's Daughter" *iPoetry*
"Like Suzanne" *Marlene in a Pub, Avalanches in Poetry*
"Little Voice Burning" *iPoetry*
"Lost in Rolling Meadows" *Intimately Intricate*
"Loud Silence" *Scribe*
"Lucid Dreams" *iPoetry, Spillwords Press*
"Makeup Heals" *iPoetry*
"Move to the Rhythm of Your Body" *Put It To Rest*
"II My Apologies, James" *Put It To Rest*
"My Lost Yoga Mat" *Put It To Rest*
"My Loyalty" *iPoetry*
"New Life" *Put It To Rest*
"Open Heart Surgery" *Put It To Rest*
"Plan Z"
"Recreate to Shed Dead Weight" *iPoetry*
"Release Me" *Put It To Rest*
"Ride at Dawn" *iPoetry*
"Scapegoat" *Put It to Rest*
"Seeing Blue Jay" *Scribe*
"Shadows of the Willow" *Intimately Intricate*
"Side Swept" *Scribe*
"Silent Dark" *iPoetry*
"Silent Loud" *iPoetry*
"Somewhere and Someplace Over the Clouds" *iPoetry*
"Stay Gold" *iPoetry*
"Stop, then Drop" *Put It To Rest*
"Sunlight" *Put It To Rest, Fine Lines Journal 32.2*
"Super Moon" *iPoetry*
"Swallowed Words Like A Baby Swallow" *Fine Lines Journal 32.3*
"The Day There Was No More Poetry" *iPoetry*
"The Dead Sea Heals All Wounds" *Put It To Rest*

The Foreword

A Perfect Moment by James Buchanan

I had a perfect moment
on a perfect day
the season was fall
the leaves were yellow
the view was perfect
and the sun was out

The music was perfect
my body and mind felt calm
I felt a perfect moment that
I thought might be
what heaven was like

I knew the moment would pass
so I appreciated every second of it
I was grateful
I was in a wonderful place
thank you
for the perfect moment.

Breaking Up With the Cobalt Blues

I Call This Trauma

The trauma unfolds
in between the folds
of the tapestry
tattooed in my living
room of silence
I howl, but nothing
comes out until a new
square weaves itself
onto there as the old
squares start to unravel
into a loose spool of thread
choking me asleep
I somehow become
emboldened in golden
and begin to look —
to actually study
how the threads morph into
knots and bows
and loops and holes
and knots and bows
and loops and holes
and knots and bows
and loops and holes...
-and forget me nots

Sometimes you make
a patchwork that
you work on tirelessly
and needlessly until
the trauma unfolds
in between the folds
of the tapestry...

...it's arduous work,
carrying this thing around
like an old wet blanket
I think I'm finally
comprehending
that it needs to be housed
in a museum and framed
and reframed and observed
and studied and, well,
displayed like an artifact
So that if and when I am forced
to confront the lava erupting
from the sleeper cell of a volcano
I can Wear it,
Speak it,
and Preserve it
I can let it hit the air
so that its power diminishes over me,
or perhaps it can be plastered
into some sort of sculpture:
a live, living vulture
to be placed on a pedestal
with the inscription
-*"I survived."*

How I Became A Poet

When my therapist
prescribed
journal writing
she said,
"I want you to journal about this."

And I replied,
"I can't;
it's too painful,
but I can write a poem."

Plan Z

For the last few years
I've been an astronaut
      spinning out through galaxies

wading through weeds of gravity
      that loses grip as I slip
back into the black abyss
      or the bottomless pit
only to drift into new galaxies
      made from old galaxies
as the old galaxy cracks or lacks
      or has an extraterrestrial attack
and I get taken out like
the fallout
      the causality
even when dressed in a hazmat

But somehow just as I almost
give into the
F
R
E
E
F
A
L
L
-I'm cradled in a net.

Cracked Voice

"You sound tired," says mom.
I can't hide when I'm beaten up
because it comes out
in my hushed, raspy voice.

When I feel so weak and alone
and when I know I'm being hurt
but keep giving up the keys
because it's in my DNA.
I find that all I can do today
is let out the screams
I suffocated into my pillow–

But when the ones
who were meant to care
are still walking wounded
and the emotional cloak
is still heavy in its absence
leaving me to wear a cloak
of smiles, lipstick, and chains
to make up for their lacking
it eventually becomes
worth my asking...

I'm cared for, aren't I?

I'm tired of all the yelling
of my cracked voice—
I have a choice
to save my voice.

It's my choice.

Fortress

Round and round the spirograph
bumping into circles
circling in
in circular motion
so fast
causing a commotion of emotions:
zigzagging, mishmashing, spiralling and mapping
all the mismatched patterns
in different colours, shades and hues
caressing my mind's war zone
until I slow the ink
and let myself think
to sink into relief
let it all spin by
hold the pen up high
choose colours with care
pen boundaries that stick
shield the pattern from smudging and running...
...Breathe...
...Touch...
...Listen...
...Taste...
...Look...
--Don't speak.

Like Rapaccini's Daughter

I wish I could tell her
it wasn't her
it didn't have anything
to do with her
it wasn't her
that he didn't love
it was himself
it wasn't her he wasn't interested in
it was himself
it wasn't her it wasn't her it wasn't her it wasn't
her fault
it was him

But
it wasn't him it wasn't him it wasn't him it was
mental illness
finding warm places in cold corridors
breaking things
not meant to be dropped
adding distorted filters
on top of pictures
shaping misshapen thought patterns
turning up in the dirty laundry, dishes, and garden...
...it was him
he couldn't stand
to live with...

The Perfect Flower

I always felt bad for the perfect flower
tall and supple
fresh, cool, and crisp
until everyone wants to take a hit
petal by petal
touch by touch
the chrysanthemum fades
stripped
from the source
-it's a perfect flower
no more

Now it's
Impure
Unsure
Spent
Soiled
Used

Preserved in a jar
no more

But there's
self-preservation

Preserve
the self
because
the world
will take
what it takes
until
there's
nothing
left
to
give.

Above the Watermark

It touched me
at the watermark
of my life, in my life, on my life
where the prints   are imprinted
as though in an album
at about that time
we even kept photo albums
in family rooms.

Yet I fought against the terrain
at what blueprints were laid
and searched for it again
there on my lips where
the confusion set in
when watching my life
unfold like a movie
with heaps of photo film
unraveling.

*(Somewhere in between
how it went, how they think it went
how it should have gone
and how it could have gone
is the real story.)*

If only my needs had come first
but at last, I'm here now
to rescue her
or it is me?

And speak for the child
who could never speak
above the watermark.

First Choice

When you stop feeling chosen
you start doing all the choosing
and become so choosy

you unchoose one by one by one by...

...and then you choose you...

the first choice
you should have made
instead of being the last choice
that's when you can finally hear
your own voice.

Sunlight

Sometimes a little bit
of sunlight goes a long way
it's like teaching teenagers
who reach for it
the rays shared over care
when I only give
a little of what I can give
to each one but it reaches
so far to such depths

Sometimes it's just a
suggestion simmering
on the surface
or a match that is lit
and then burns
for eternity

Like my grade 8
English teacher
Ms. Pitcairn
who gave a little
-that meant a lot.

Friendships Sail

There should be a shrine
to put remnants inside of people
dead or alive that faded and stayed
waited and abated that used and abused
gifted and entrusted
that loved the most fragile of parts
with the most brokenness of hearts
in the creases of my memories
are those friendships that jumped ship
sank or swam and set sail

It doesn't matter who was driving
it's still a messy bed
and back shed
of crushed dandelions
rose-gold petals
stones and earth
encrusted in thick blades
of sweet grass and
leaves of grass
winding onto paths

Sometimes you step on a blade
it's soft inside
velvety and kind
other steps are like shards
of grassy glass
cutting into muscle mass

But I can't do the math
it's all in the past we had a blast
there were highs and there were lows
a holding of hands and twisted souls
only you and I know
sometimes I wish you didn't have to go
or that I didn't have to let you go
~ *I just wanted you to know.*

Just Out of Touch

Just out of touch
(I miss it so much)
The rhythm of the day
(I knew just what to say)
I knew my way from the way
the time and the day
It all had a time and a place
a purpose and a routine

Like rearranging and redecorating
Except for every time I look for comfort
The lights go on or off

And the monsters under the bed
rear their ugly Medusa head
I dream of a time when I floated
on a magic carpet ride to take the tide

Full of some spontaneity
Like when you would bump into someone
locally and other times even overseas

But now it's just a mazy haze of moving through
our days in all of these disenchanted ways

Spending time in the spellbound
cyberspace and in between
space of living with this new normal.

like a paper cut

invisible
yet
visible

when
a
slow
drip
drip
drip
drop

dribbles
leaks
and then streaks
crimson onto white
painless and yet painful
like a passing thought or
an unkind word that you
forgot until a tear appears
and reappears in the shape
of a shapeshifting tear
stain on the heart

—like a
paper
cut.

Unrecognizable

You build yourself
one brick
at a time
to make yourself
only to break yourself
as quickly as a wine
glass tumbles to the floor

All that pouring, all that tending, all that washing,
all that mending, all that drying, all that shining
to only fall-shattering—
unrecognizable

Sure, you can glue it back together
but will it show? will it glitter? will it glow?
will it hold after the next glass has been poured?

drip
      drip
           drip
   drop

When all you want to do is guzzle...
A gazillion, tiny, small, frail pieces
smash—
unrecognizable
Where did you all go?
You used to want to dress me in Cab Merlot

Catch up to My Feelings

Sometimes my feelings
need to catch up to me
first I can't feel
I go on as I was
because I can't heal
upon the sudden kneel
I can't make it a big deal
for some reason, it's never ideal
to feel
I need to first eat a meal
let it catch up
to me
sometimes it even
sneaks up
on me
like a strain of cannabis creeper.

At first, I run away
no time to contain
the pain
no need to name
then the feelings
catch up
to catch them
in an
o
v
e
r
f
l
o
w

i
n
g
cup.

Then come out alive
on the other side.

Eyes wide open
like Baby Alive.

A Hummingbird Sang For Me Today

Dedicated to mi abuela Simy

A hummingbird sang for me today
the bearer of good news they say
it fluttered this way and that way
back and forth, and side to side
like a swing suspended in time
floating there, chirping a few feet away
it spoke to me today
any minute now the joy is meant to sing
and hum a new tune
by tuning the untuned into the tuned
it sang anew
the hummingbird sang
the hummingbird sang for me today
the bearer of good news they say.

Like A Muse In A Cage

Like a muse in a cage
like a punk in a midnight choir
I have tried in my way to be free.

Like a ballerina teetering on a music box
like a skunk stuck in an hour
I have tried in my way to be free.

Like an aloof armadillo in an explosion
like a translucent paper nautilus exposed
I have tried in my way to be free.

But even when my heart spills
like black squid ink upon a page
my essence remains chained.

But you swore on that song
and all you had done wrong
that you would make it up to me.
You said that together we would be free.

But the world's handprints are still on me.

Like Suzanne

I always wanted to be like Suzanne
feeding men tea and oranges
by the river like a siren
or one of Cohen's lovers
shacked up in Hydra
like the Paris ex-pats buzzing around
abstract words and images.
But then that would somehow mean
that I would also be in love
with a man who struggled to love
because he struggled to love himself.
But does that matter?

Does it matter
that he didn't love in their way
in the right way
but in his way
and was it not better than no way.
Is it not
better to have loved and lost
than never to have loved at all?
I still want to be Suzanne
free to love
how and whomever
she wants
because she's tameless
and irresistible...

Scapegoat

I've never been the darling
or the fan favourite

I was never given anything
I didn't earn

I was only given things
I never asked for

or never wanted
because

I'm the truth-teller
and no one likes
to hear
the truth.

I: Carving Space for You

You still have a hold
on me, in me, around
me, about me, and for me

Even though our story
ended in a plot
twist
leaving me
twisted
like twigs at the bottom
of a soggy sandbox
discarded like children's
shovels and pails
full of *what was*
what wasn't and *what-ifs*

Sometimes you're
unearthed
like Spring
the month *it*
happened —
April
and those
showers, those
April showers
startle me
when I'm faced
with stories of...
...*Suicide*...

there — I said it
I breathed it:
Suicide.

But our conversation
does not end
there
it writes itself
and unfolds in
the folds of the living
crossing over
borders
in memories
like some distant
reverie
unearthed on this earth
in moments of stillness
and movement
in times of sadness
and joy

That Spring
when it became your
winter and my
fall
from a shroud
of innocence
until my bones
melted into
and surrendered
to the hot

yoga mat
that filtered out
the whispers
of reasons and explanations
from the other side:
where we wonder
gasp and grasp
at the dots that need
connecting.

I still hold space
for you
a sacred space
in eternal space

I carved it out for you
the one you chose to hold.

II: My Apologies, *James*

You asked me what I thought
of people who committed suicide:
being in my early 20s,
I parroted my mother's words
and proclaimed that it was *"selfish."*

You were kind of haunted by my response —
offended almost.

*(Like the time I asked you
about that family member in the photo
and you turned away in shame
as I was witnessing your pain.)*

For a split second, it stopped me,
but then I washed the dirt all away...
I can tackle it another day, *I thought*,
as I wrapped myself in a warm,
wool shawl of innocence...

...But now I know that those
invasive, pervasive thoughts and feelings
were like live-wired and hard-wired
seething pain electrocuting you
slowly into submission.

I only discovered what I assumed
was your first suicide attempt,
a few months after calling you my own.

Then, when you told me you had recovered,

I believed you because I wanted to.
"He must be over it," I mused.

It wasn't until life had collapsed in on itself
in my late 30s, while watching *13 Reasons Why*
when I realized that *it* never goes away
— *of course, I thought* — it's an ongoing battle...

Suddenly my darting thoughts turned to you
but then I must have been swallowed up
by life again because I never followed my hunch
instead, I puked up my lunch...

"It's not selfish," James.
"I'm sorry."
"Can you ever forgive me?"

III: Your Suicide By My Side, Looming Like an Albatross

I am not okay —
I am forever changed
and it just happens
to be my favourite season
— spring —
birthdays for my boys and husband
and now you...
your suicide by my side,
looming like an albatross

That's my life —
that's my pain
and if mine is so great
then what must yours
have been like
Sorry, I guess I was selfish
for not staying in touch
but neither did you
and then you had to go
and make it all final

Now that Instagram post —
"Awaiting Fireworks" —
the one that compelled you
to tell me that I still looked
the same —
that's the last thing you said to me

But I still have some questions for you...
that poem you sent me —
"A Perfect Moment" —
Are you in it now?

Did you find that eternal moment?
And what's in a moment?
Because that was our moment
and before I knew it
a moment turned into two years
(I swear I was just tying my shoes
and I must have looked
down for too long...)
when all I heard was a thunderclap
that Saturday morning
while scrolling my newsfeed
in the midst of mixing pancake batter
amongst my baby's and children's
clatter and chatter

(But it didn't matter
all I could see was you...
your suicide by my side,
looming like an albatross.)

Life in Quarantine

There is a silent enemy
seeping into
our borders
our homes
our bodies
our lungs
travelling at high-speed
dividing us, while it divides, doubles,
triples, quadruples...multiplies...
showing our humanity or inhumanity:
hoarders, villains, heroes & martyrs
Except our call of duty isn't combat
it's called "social distancing"
a codeword for the interruption
of our daily lives
Palms and faces pressed up
against windows
donning drawings of rainbows
While healthcare workers
hand us life-preservers
as we race to preserve life
arming up against this virus
that we can't debug
wiping countries clean
And we crown those who have never been crowned
until
"Corona"
became a household name
Our call of duty is here:

dividing us into isolation
with reverberations
settling into our foundation
Uprooting our past, present & future
Staining our family portraits
Draining our finances
And when we walk out the front door:
everyone is suspect —
friends, family, neighbours—
as it spreads like a wildfire
with too many hotspots to douse
We're living inside a dystopian novel
like Julia and Winston
sharing a kiss and chocolate
in solidarity in the dark
via a sort of morse code:
1-2-3 #Covid19
4-5-6 #SocialDistancing
8-9-10 #FlatteningtheCurve
Because now it's here —
not just over there
not just "near"
not just something you hear
We are chasing you
trying to corner you
to isolate the contagion
but you're invisible
some even think they are invincible
It's as futile as swatting a fly
But still we buy time
as you suffocate some of us

that is until your time runs out
and we smother you and Rise
(though right now it's still all too much to surmise)
Because some world leaders are stalling
like a bad rendition of *Hamlet*
Something is rotten in this global village
and it's not as simple as
the plague of Thebes:
there is no Oedipus to exile
no Oracle or Blind Prophet
or is there?
We struggle to awaken
from drowning in the pages of this dystopia but
it's like a broken vinyl on repeat
skipping and scratching
scratching and skipping
while babies are born in quarantine
and the dead die alone
Will we ever dance in tune again?

Lucid Dreams

The time between the first and second lockdown
was like a lucid dream:
awake but not awake
dreaming but not dreaming
in control and out of control
sleeping and awakening
aware and unaware
knowing and not knowing
looking and finding
healing and mending
masking and unmasking
waiting and starting
stopping and going
Now that we're in the thick of the fog again
I can't remember what that dream was all about
it was like a pause except it wasn't a pause
it was a life ~ on hold ~
learning new dreams to dream:
how to hold them
how to own them
how to remember them
how to share them
(dreams that is...)
-Lucid Dreams.

Find Something You Love

"Find something you love"
I found myself saying to my 12-year-old
anything will do
just something
to put your mind to
and put everything
on the line for
and not give up on
for anyone
not even you.

A craft that you can craft
where you don't need a map
but there's no looking back.

Something to lose yourself in
and find yourself in
both at the same time.

Truth Teller

I don't need
anyone to validate
my words
as if to stamp
each letter
pause, and period
because
poetry is still poetry
whether published
in the New Yorker
or tucked away
in an abandoned journal
in a sock drawer

When I'm the one
who lived the experience
whether the truth unfolded
linear or nonlinear
or I told it
backward or forward
sideways or upside down
does not change
what happened

So take care of you
and be well
Sorry, not sorry
that my story
forces you

to change your life story
but that's none of my concern.

Signed,
Truth Teller.

Like An Iceberg

Sometimes growth is more like an iceberg —
doing all the growing

Underwater

    — until it floats

back on up

to the top.

Release Me

Release me from the woman
they wanted me to be
Release me of the woman they see
Release me from the woman
dressed in their insecurities
Release me of the woman they see

When they hold their own mirror
in front of me and tell me
to repeat their story of fragility
like a puppet on a string
to suit their agenda
and the narrative
that has infected
critical thinking

There's no more divergent thinking
and yet conspiracy theories run around
with credibility
Everything is debatable
except what's important to me

*Why is it that it's always okay
to tell me what my story is?
But I should somehow paint my world
in their stories?*
I am not a colonizer
even though you want me to be...

That is not my story as you colonize
my body, heart, mind, and soul...
(But I am a descendant of grandparents
who fled their homes due to persecution)
Release me from the woman
they want me to be
Release me of the woman they see
Release me from the woman
dressed in their insecurities
Release me of the woman they see

How to Live

1. Be Too Much

Be
Too
Much.

Rise
Up
with the cheers.

Pay no mind
to the jeers.

But most of all
-Be sincere.

2. Live Out Loud

Live
Out
Loud.

Through love
through fear
through silence.

So that others
can live
out loud too.

When You Step Off The Ride

When you step off the ride
and there's nowhere to hide
in the thickets and pickets of your mind
because you bought a new ticket —
a new ticket to ride

When something or someone
has a hold on you
and dopamine plays a role
taking total control
and takes its toll
and makes you pay
an endless toll
— it all looks so basic
when you're off the hook
and the party is all done
and it's just you
cleaning up the confetti
empties and wannabees
or the fallen feathers
that were plucked
from the boa
just discarded there
on the carpet
— *lifeless*

Like the time when
I was only 17
and raves and my friends

were everything
until the dusty pink
sun rose
and streaks of light
replaced the blinding strobe lights
in the lonely warehouse
over the docks
of Lake Ontario
or the time I was
a travel bug
all hopped up on hope
and wanderlust
until the moving around
became work
and all I wanted was
to feel the earth
beneath my feet

Or when I wanted to be lost
in the desire to burn thermal fires
it didn't matter
if he or she was a liar
when all that mattered
was getting higher

Until, eventually, I wanted to feel
eventually, I want to heal
ultimately, it was more hurtful
to run away and stay
than it was to flourish.

Like A Glitzy Dress on A Hanger

Maybe you don't really know
what it's like
to drag your body around
like a glitzy dress on a hanger
or a black-and-white portrait
of a lady with an absent smile
or wrinkled linen on a washboard.

But when you grew up
seeing what other grown women do
it's not easy to be a new you.

Like the woman who only granted herself
such small portions of nutrients
because she survived portioned life
in the Transnistria ghetto.
*(But she always had a dark chocolate bar
or Swedish berries stashed away — just for me.)*

Or the woman who served her family
as though they were seated at a banquet
but there was never any time to eat
when she was the belle of the ball.
*(But she always had a second serving
of vegetable or chicken soup — just for me.)*

Or the almond mom who never noticed
when you lived on a health bar
because she was a health nut

that made you nuts
by making sure you knew
Twiggy was cool
when Marilyn was your sweet tooth truth.
(But she always did have another health bar — just
for me.)

But today,
there is no one here to give me
what is left.
Instead, the dull aching birth
of a migraine took the win
when I listened
to my tingling feet and hands
and said "fuck it" to my plans.
And made myself
a warm salted bath
for my reverberating limbs
because sometimes
"rest"
is what the body says
when it refuses to get dressed.
And you give your body
and their bodies
the "rest"
a woman deserves.

The rest that doesn't always
have to be earned
as you welcome her
like a *Shabbat Queen.

- The name means Queen of the Sabbath, and the entity is the personification of the Jewish day of rest, Saturday. She still possesses a prominent position in Judaic mythology.

Open Heart Surgery

Open heart surgery
is what it was like
when my heart burst open
like shards of glass
from the past —
out at last
when life was like a ballerina
teetering on the edge
of the music box
going fast
then slow
never letting go
falling off though
when it rocks slow...
slowly, slowly spinning
spinning out, flipping out, stepping out
into a history of missteps that
stepped that same steps
of heartache
carried through
who would have known
all the hearts that need to be let go
to let it go
and grow
there in the cold pain
is the calm after the rain
but is it calm
or is it numb
and maybe even dumb
to love again
to trust again
to travel together again
in no man's land.

Every Rose Has A Thorn

Every rose
has a thorn, and yet
remains eternal
in its grace.
That's why the mirror
with the engraved rose
weathering
and not withering
just fluttering,
simply dropping
and hanging on,
left a stain
on my
heart.
It was placed
in our home
overtop
the mantle
even
though
our hearts
were bleeding
like bleeding hearts
in
the
garden
to
hide
the
ugly
with
the
beauty
of a

single,
silent
dusty pink
rose.

The mirror became a point of contention: *just another beauty to resent.* So beautiful and yet so tragic when all that it touches it pricks — *a self-fulfilling prophecy.*

Is the rose too perfect? Or must it stand alone in her birthright? The birthright they stole from her, as they stripped her of her thorns.

And preserved her in glass with no air to breathe in a museum. Just like the rose in *The Little Prince.*

There's a reason every rose has its thorn, and yet is eternal in its grace. It's because every rose has its thorn.

It's whether or not you still smell it, water it, feed it, adorn it, and display it when it pricks. That's what makes it unconditional, *isn't it?* Or is it?

Which one is it? The rose or the thorn? Do you have to accept one to accept the other?

A single, silent, dusty pink rose, that is. Because *"a rose by any other name would smell as sweet."*

Give and Take

That which was stolen from you
that you gave in good faith
only to have it thrown in your face
will that priceless love ever be returned
or robbed for good in bad faith
leaving a gaping wound in its festering place

Only time will tell how that lost time will turn out
but something tells me if it's anything like real life
it will end in a shitty way because death always
brings out the worst in people
isn't just something they say

Can time be returned
the first-time ever relearned
love ever really earned
Maybe you don't count
what you gave
you don't regret
the love you gave

Instead, you say —
they must have really needed it...
and sit peacefully with the unconditional love
you gave away.

I Butterflies In My Belly

I know it sounds strange maybe a bit deranged
but when I'm a healthy weight that
means I'm happy.
Even though I try to tell myself
that those times
I couldn't eat
because the butterflies
took up so much space
the truth is
that when I feed myself
nourishment
of love, food, and truth
I am most happy.
I've been feeding myself more liberally
and so the butterflies have departed
they fluttered away beautifully
leaving hunger in its wake —
no more belly aches.

II Butterflies In Their Bellies

I don't know what I would say
to my daughter
But I know that already
I speak to my sons
with more empathy

I notice when feelings
drown the body
and when they don't eat
as much because
they have butterflies in their belly
or when they eat too much
to keep the butterflies
down
I try not to be one of those moms
but it fell out of my mouth, *it did...*

"You're looking a little skinny," I said
but I met that with
"You had a hard week"
and *"it's okay*
you will pack it back on."

The butterflies had their way
with you this week
but it doesn't mean
they will feed on you next week
when you settle them
with nourishment.

My Lost Yoga Mat

I found what I was looking for
on my lost yoga mat.
It was buried in the basement
(lost in the move)
Carelessly thrown into a hockey bag.
"I need to find my yoga mat," I would say.
Then another day and another day would pass.
Sometimes I had an "ask" in me
other times I didn't want to see
what happened to the real me
there on the yoga mat
are all the things you can take back...
All the gifts
good and bad
I never asked for
but was given.
Maybe it's time I regift them
send them out on their merry way
with my breath today ...

Bleeding Hearts

When
raindrops
keep
falling on my
head like every word
that was ever said and ever
cried or was crying and ever lied
or was lying and ever died or was dying...
But as long as you're trying your best right?
(What if your best just isn't good enough?)
What about when you seem to lose care?
(Does that mean you're
undeserving of care?)
So let the rain fall
in the open air
and seep deep
into the blades
of sweet
green
grass
caressing
the
smooth,
jagged,
and
jaded
edges
of
our
bleeding hearts

When the Landscape Drifts

When the landscape drifts
when the past shifts
when those around you
shapeshift and switch.
How do you find a fit?
That perfect near miss
when the landscape drifts
because it slides
before your dusty eyes
floating there by the sea.

Floating there by the sea
before your dusty eyes
because it slides
when the landscape drifts
that perfect near miss.
How do you find a fit?
Shapeshift and switch
when those around you
when the past shifts
when the landscape drifts.

When Purple Rain Is Falling

When purple rain
is falling, falling,
dropping, fast,
furious, and then
slowly
maybe even a bit
deliriously
from the open sky...
Letting it all out
just you,
the little old world,
and I.
That's when we find
it's okay to say
let's go crazy
despite the tsunami
elevator we ride
up and down
side to side
but that doesn't mean
we have to slide.

When the Sun Rose

When I woke you
to say I couldn't sleep
and we both knew our souls
needed to eat
We talked on the porch
as the sun rose
like we did when we first
discovered our thirst
when we couldn't stand
to be away from one another
so we held on so fiercely
that when life pierced us
we decided not to let it
define us or own us
but to greet the dawn
because the sun still rose
Like the black rose
of a new dawn
in the middle of the night.

Black Light Dragonfly

I thought that maybe something shifted
when we finally took one another out
of the small peg we had shoved ourselves into
like a middle school locker
(the one you kissed me in front of).

Now that we've unraveled the chains
tied around us they've split apart
and ripped up and through
our junkyard and jukebox of love
(taking me back to you and me,
and a kitchen sink at *Lime Rickey's).*

But as we married our lights and our darks
and tried to separate the lights from the darks
it all came undone when there was an electric spark
buzzing around the pebbled shores of Cape Cod
that August when we were born.

Can we use the chains as a link?
Or maybe a fun new kink?
and know when nothing is the way it was
it's because we found a new door
one that adores our ugliest sides so hard
they cascade like a dragonfly lighting up the sky
in cracks of green, mauve, and fluttering black light

Because, despite its sting,
she's still beautiful when she sings...

I've Climbed Mountains

I've climbed mountains no one can see
gotten back up with scraped knees
fallen off a few cliffs, walked over the cliff
and even had others throw me from the cliff
But staying in that struggle
is not where my heart wants to go...
as I hurl the dead weight over the ledge

Because now it's time to let go
and release all that I've buried
Sail off into the sunset
we all deserve it — the view that is
from the top of the mountain
at sunrise or sunset

Have you ever witnessed such grace
when the sunlight hits your face?

Those orange sherbet blast sunrises
live inside of me now
because they set there
from Santorini to Pesaro
from Jerusalem to Mount Masada
from Mount Sinai to the Pyramids of Giza
all the way through the Samaria Gorge
to end up by the Libyan sea

I've climbed mountains no one can see
but why is it that no one reminded me
just how sweet the descent can be
when you set yourself free.

A Love Letter To Montreal

When you're a poet
you fall in love with cities
Montreal was one of my lovers
A young lover
Of adventure, passion, culture and freedom
Of curiosity, arts and societies
Of universities, pubs, dorms, cafés and libraries
A time when there was so much in front of me
and I never would have imagined
that I could achieve it all
so clumsily
or sporadically
when I envisioned it all
so gracefully
and linear...
but like an old lover
Montreal will always have an imprint on me.

When She's Lost and Then Found

When she's lost and then found
Do you think she wants to tell everyone why she was
lost?
Do you think she wants her story plastered on social
media
like her missing face was?
Do you think that the story
is just so simple?
"Mental illness they say"
Is that it? Is that all?
Because she's not just some missing person
I knew her as a little girl
I knew her as an open-hearted youth
I knew her then
I knew her when...
Life moved at such a different pace
and we all knew a friendly face
She is from that time and place
I wonder if she lost herself somewhere in there?
I want her to know I see her
and I hope she recovers
Even though she probably wants to live
under
the covers.

Grief

There was a life lived
in a language of youthful innocence
we spoke but then we both awoke
after weathering more of life.

This morsel of time is only a memory
that passed in time
and yet who you and I were
also unlocks an "I" that is no more
only you knew that version of me.

Maybe there's a key in there still
A key to open the light that you shone
even when you may have not had light left for you.

A light that lives on in your memory.

You Were Too Good For Us

You were too good for this world
we couldn't understand you
the way you needed to be understood
and yet understood us all

You remind us of what is broken
How much is broken
When you broke right along with it all

Today, I am broken
Maybe tomorrow I will pick up a piece
but for now
I hold all the broken pieces
and just accept
that they are
broken.

The Deep Freeze

There is a deep freeze within me
it moved in swiftly and yet slowly
blanketing me in black ice
my body is still
frozen against my will
fear gripping it still
though my hot breath
moves like quicksand
it's not enough to revive my eyes
now fluttered and shuttered
from the weight of the windchill
that clings to my bones...
It's been so long that now the ice feels like home.

It Was Never A Big Deal

It was never a big deal
I had to tell myself to survive
It would all somehow get swept up
or swept aside
amongst the dresses and the jewels
or the dinners with company
But within those confines
were so many lines
crossed, tossed, and lost
There where you never felt safe
when there's a shoe waiting to drop
maybe even handmade
That's all I can say
that it's buried in there somewhere
the gnawing pain
that lashes me
because it was lashed out on me.

I Tripped on a Wound Today

I didn't think I was going to participate in today's prompt. After trying to decide which scab I would pick away at, or pick at to explore the topic of healing, I got tired, so I decided the task was too much for me today. *But I'm afraid the task found me.*

You see I'm walking, walking wounded now.

My intergenerational trauma wound is showing: it was exposed, punctured, and is gushing blood into puddles on the floor of my heart, and on the helm of my soul.

The story's title *Channeling my Inner Anne Frank in a Pandemic* followed by a correction from the Twitter feed of the SS in Germany aka *The Globe and Mail* who said they were making a "clarification"—not an "apology" but a correction, that the story should read *Lessons in Living from Anne Frank.*

I'm walking, walking wounded now.

I'm sorry bubby Toby, you were right: they hate us, they always have and always will.

I'm sorry bubby, your family died in vain.

I'm sorry bubby, your baby was six months old in the ghettos of Transnistria.

I'm sorry bubby: your 12-year-old niece, Erika, was shot to death in a pogrom. I could still see the pain in your crystal blue fairy eyes, shooting an image at me in the reflection of your stunned pupils.

I'm sorry bubby, I'm sorry.

I'm sorry time plays tricks on us so that the most wretched parts of history seem like fiction.

And I'm so sorry Anne. I'm so sorry that people suck. I walked through the attic where you hid when I toured Amsterdam and reveled at your small statue in the square. I know it's still there. Anne, if you're listening, it's okay, but it isn't okay. It's not okay. I'm not okay. *We're not okay.*

I tripped on a wound today.

Stop, then Drop

In fleeting moments
that pace is mine
it reminds me of a life
of a time that echoes
in hope,
belonging
community
balance
harmony
between us
you and me
me and you,
and all we do

But these days there is so
much chaos
gridlock
hip
then
hop
— *stop*
then
drop.

The Innocent

When the child becomes
an adult only to discover
the adult was the real
child and that the
accomplices were
complicit ...
Only then —
right there
Will you be forced
to face
your two-face

*Can you even
look at it
any longer?*

When reality
catches up to you
and snags you so
so you can no longer
wag your finger
or wage your war
on an innocent

*Who is left to name
in your blame
game?*

Cruising

Life keeps taking me
in many different
directions
All at the same time
Pulling me in ways
that can't be pulled
When all I want to do
is direct traffic...
But it keeps steering me
stalling me, hijacking me
stealing me, or crashing me

When will I cruise again?

New Life

When your own little world
becomes unrecognizable ...

Do you form anew to reconnect
or cling to death for life?

Turning Back Shadows

Is it okay to admit
I'm casting a spell
to cast buckets of water
to turn back those
shadows of doubt
to rekindle trust?

Is it okay to admit
we flamed those fires
and went feeding them
coal instead of mending
the broken holes?

Beyond the shadows of doubt
is no doubt there are layers
of unraveling and unpacking
to patch and rebuild
something that holds — still
to still hold all of the exposed
holes in our souls.

Is it okay to admit
when the shit
hits the fan
there's nowhere
left for it to land
but in our laps?

And you need to turn off
all the noise to find the pace
that never replaces
two hearts intertwined
in chapters and verses
footnotes and endnotes
sequels and outtakes.
Is it okay to admit
that we asked for help?

The pile became too much
to sort, purge, cleanse and stock
without taking stock of all that stalks
us with the need to talk.

Come Undone

The snaps have been snap snapping
so much just keeps happening   happening
unpredictable   predictability   has found
the key to my home

When I managed to ward off the wolf
who waltzed through our front doors
even when we brandished it with
an evil eye or a decadent chunk of Turkish delight
in a moment of flight
soaring above worry and doubt

Is where truths finally come out
swimming like the tiger-eyed sun
setting in the November sky
playing November raindrops
as all of the desperation and disguises
purge out of the treasure box

Because the deeper the dirt
the more golden the heart
the fiery-fierce the passion
the more down and low the sorrow
In all of the rooms of the house:
the foyer, the basement, the encasement
to the bedroom, and the attic too
so many parts, and chapters
and hearts, cutting rocks in the dark

Blazing light on wounds
nearly fresh, just made razor-sharp
by a stinging reminder
like nicking yourself in the shower

Yes, sometimes love is friends with hate
and it takes you on a bad date, sometimes
the two can relate, especially when love
was always served up to you in this way

But I have to keep thinking that there is a way to
find a better way, and how way leads on to way, and
how each day has been spent with you and that our
ways must lead back to the best way — the only way
— *and so I pray* that this all comes undone.

It's A Love-Hate Thing

The fine line between love and hate
can blur so much it makes you fascinate
when you love so hard
you hate because
you hate to be vulnerable
and you love to hate
or hate to be loved
or hate to love
and so you hate what you love
and love what you hate
but then how can it be
any different because you only hate
what you care about
and so you can't love what you can't hate
but you can hate what you can't love.

Untangling New Roots

The next time you put down new roots
make sure they don't get entangled with
or tangled up in decay or end up hanging on the
hook.
Those roots you dug up uprooted like a turnip
turned upside down that you had to babysit
as others bloomed...
...You've been roaming
the lost and found as though awaiting
a messenger, clutching bulbs of fresh dirt
like Ophelia muttering
on the meaning of madness
with a rosary and wreath of roses
while everyone lights her on fire.
But now the time is on the horizon
the garden awaits the hands that held on
to hope in outer space now caress your face
submerged in the salt of the earth
— the mud of the Dead Sea.
Your ancestors traveled arduous treks
carried roots only to replant them miles away
oceans away, cultures away.
What would they think
of your 40-mile migration?
Then again, people today
sure do have a lot to say
about unearthing yourself
one by one, brick by brick.

So maybe there was never
a little earthquake that came for them again
(here we go again) that spun them out
into a painfully familiar
tailspin like a fishtail
into a black hole
so far from home
that you had no other choice
but to hear your own voice
beckoning you to keep going
to keep growing.

What's It All For?

I beat you up,
try my luck,
play it safe
drag you out
on more than
one bad date
throw you in heels
dip you in wine
say it's no big deal
also, skip some meals
Then I kept it all inside
with shallow breaths
sometimes making me
so dizzy, it's hard to breathe
This shell I am in
is paper-thin
when I am wearing
as thin as the top
layer of a nougat bar
slowly peeling
like my loins — so groggy
from all of the noise
Was life always this heavy?
Was I always this heavy?
There were heavy times
but now so much weighs on the mind
all of the time —
adulting is such hard work
no wonder I escape

and then I'm left to wonder
what I did while escaping...
Did I take care of you?
Or abuse you some more?
-*What's it all for?*

Know Your Worth

It made you feel worthless
But It didn't change your worth
~ For what it's worth ~

When I Climb Back Out of the Darkness

When I climb back out of the dark
I will remember just who it was who held my hand
When I climb back out of the dark
I will remember just who it was who lit a match
When I climb back out of the dark
I will remember just who tried to bury me alive
When I climb so high that I ascend through another
life lesson,
to marry my darkness within the light that has been
born
once again, like beauty and her beast
we will rejoice in this marriage of light and dark
death and start, life and ends
But just don't ever tell me you know how my story
ends
And never assume that your story is done,
maybe it hasn't even begun
What will you look like when the darkness comes for
you?
Will you know just what to do?
Or has it been so long since you knew what resilience
or discomfort mean?
Because sometimes we only return home
after defeating Calypso like Odysseus
to have to then face all that has changed
and all that remains
When I climb back out of the dark
I will remember just who it was who held my hand
and who counted me for dead.

The Sweet November Rain

Remember when we
used to listen to
the sweet November rain
and we knew nothing from pain
only French kisses
that ignited a young love
that grew ever so slowly
from seed to bud to leaf
to flower, all in very
long, yet short hours.
Only to create a Garden
of Eden that we honoured
tended and adored
like under an open roof
courtyard on Loganberry
never ever feeling alone
because while there is always
rain in November, it's still sweet
like the wonderous passages
inroads, and even potholes
of you and me
and all we ever were
are, could, and will be.
I love you like the sweet November rain
it is a love that will never fade
even when our youthfulness may.

All I ask is that you remind me
of who I was then — *okay?*

Closer to Truth

When you lose someone
not only do you lose them
but then you are reminded of the person
they hoped you would be
and then when you stop to look
and ask yourself if you're all those things —
even if you're all those things and more

Why is it that you don't feel it's ever good enough?

Is it because if you were to live by their honour,
you would have to face some hard truths?

Just how much closer to truth
will the loss of a loved one
make you become?

I Will Remember

I will remember, I will remember, I will remember
as soon as I get out of here
as soon as I can stand
as soon as I can talk
as soon as it stops

I will remember, I will remember, I will remember
as soon as I wake up
as soon as I know how
as soon as I get out
as soon as my body returns

But it was my mind
that never returned
when he tucked my body back
ever so gently
into my bed in the dormitory
like a friend caring for me
with a hangover
at the time I must have been
reading Dante's purgatory

When memory was like
a lost email
an address not found
undeliverable
in the drafts
or the unsent box
just waiting for me
to be able to read it

Until that scene in the movie
pressed send
and sent the memory back to me
like a message
sending my body back to me
(I will remember, I will remember, I will remember)
I kept saying to myself
— only it took all these years
to hear, see, taste and smell
what happened to me

I will remember, I will...remember...
the belt buckle jingling
the tick-tocks tingling
the ice in the drink
that my friend mixed
clink-clinking

Thank you memory
for protecting me
because I felt nothing
and I still feel nothing
except for disbelief
at how my mind
protected me.

I will remember
the silent and confusing
silence and confusion —
hovering over my frozen body.
Do you feel me?

Little Voice Burning

Her little voice
could not be heard
(not even amongst blackbirds
Or was it Blue Beard?)
little she spoke
little she woke
little she supposed
while being made to hold
the same pose
like a little lady
who dared not complain
hands crossed on her tainted lap
her lips drawn up in a smile
breaking from the weight
of the flimsy threads and knots
threading her lips red
an innocence taken
right there before them
reading all of her signals wrong
and letting it go
as they let her go
as she let the memory
fade to the back pocket
of her mind
where no one
not even her
would think to find
(They like her better
when their comfort comes first
was what it was like
on her burning insides...)

Ride At Dawn

She begged her to save her
or herself or her and herself
or was it herself
to make an example
to set the example
but she wouldn't
draw that line in the sand
she wouldn't or couldn't
put it down or drop it down
When she looked for protection
she would not or could not afford
she felt so helpless as she struggled
to maintain control of the discord
and some semblance of law and order
in the disordered living room
While watching her fawn
until it all dawns on her at dawn
and compels her to move on
to stay strong —
but for how long?
to what end? to what cost?
If all is lost...
They say that true companionship
is being prepared to do whatever it takes
one lights the match and the other rides at dawn
and even if she needed to light her own match
it's better to be her own companion than
to carry a foe, so she dried out the matchsticks and
found her red dancing shoes.

Somewhere and Someplace Over the Clouds

when they scatter me in clouds
to cloud my vision
if I am the sun
and dress me up in ribbons
only to tie me down in them
and then run away
the stronger my sun rays reach
sometimes it almost seems
the darker the clouds hover
to cast dark shadows over sparkling jewels
— Jungian shadows, I've found —
buried deep, deep, deep
down
are there to teach
That's why I had to climb many mountains
to a place where
there are no clouds
to live above the clouds
somewhere over the clouds
to sing: I made it aloud!
to be the sun and meet the sun
when they scatter clouds my way
to only sit back to greet the day
the way I used to escape by making shapes in clouds.

Upside Down and Inside Out

Life has been turned
upside down
like an upside-down cake
that did not rise
or a lemon cake that is too tart
the art of living has died
and there is nowhere to hide
the fools have pride
that's taking us on a ride
from defunding libraries
and funding guns
to outlawing women
from owning bodily autonomy
the inside-out world
has taken hold of us
and you and me and everybody
when knowledge is power
and they want to keep us
down in an endless loop
of wanting just an hour
spinning out and running out
to work for the machine
instead of humanity.

Silent Loud

It's been silently loud
and loudly silent
silent loud
and loud silence
some may even call it
mad science
when you're curing
broken spirits
to curate artistry from pain
after wandering
in the silently loud rain
but instead of tripping on a trigger
you choose to see the glimmer
in shining a light on silent loud
it shouts out the shouts of silence
— until the silence isn't so loud anymore.

Silent Dark

Is it just me
or so it seems
that women and children
pay for men's sins
Like a bad episode
of Adam and Eve
it's an epidemic
around here
near and far
and here and there
and everywhere —
no, the kids are not okay
and neither are
the men and women
Yes, I say this
on International Women's Day
It's time to quit toxic masculinity
exploiting women's bodies
because it's not just women
it's families who break

~~~~

apart

~~~~

at the tug of the
heart
in the silent
dark
At least that's what
some of my students say

when they share
the darkness
until it becomes less silent.

Loud Silence

When someone who
is supposed to know you
someone who
once knew you
like the back of your hand
or a favourite pink pashmina
or a ballerina teetering on top
of a music box
suddenly doesn't look at you
or look like you remember
when you know parts
of them fester
and you're met in superficial
gestures
while they judge and whisper
to keep you
at a distance
behind some distorted image
of who they think you are
to protect themselves.
Do you even remember
who I am?
Because you're all the things
you said
you would never be
all the things you
pretend not to be
as you erase
you and me.

A New Day

When the sun greets
a new day
and the old day
and old ways
give way
When the loops
stop looping
and the changes
start changing
when the friction is shifting
Is it fact
or is it fiction?
When the dawn
greets the evening
and the set
meets the sun at sunset
Is it night
or is it day?
Is it birth
or is it death?
Is it time
to finally forgive
and forget?
Or do we forgive
and live and let live
or put it to rest?
When spring gives way
to a sunless winter
where this winter was

like one long day
or one long night
that was out of sight
but now by now
the night has broke —
the fast is over the sun rejoices
flashing light
on better choices
and empowered voices.

Like A Fault Line

It cut you —
right to the very
heart of you
in the place
that leaves a trace
even when you tried
so hard to erase
what you could not understand
but when the senses
couldn't make sense
it left a gaping wound
in the room of your betrayed heart
the only difference is —
some things can be healed
and others birth a scar:
like a fault line
that runs so deep
it doesn't make a sound
until it creeps
back into you
even in your sleep...

Dancing Through the Dark

Dancing in the dark
Dancing through the dark
Dancing with the dark
Dancing out the dark.

It Doesn't Make You Ugly

We don't want to talk about how badly we've
been hurt
because we figure if we've been hurt
so much we must have been defective
or at least we must be that defective now.

We don't want anyone to see
how they treated us
or when we gave them the gun.

It's time to accept the hurt happened.
And to know it doesn't make you ugly.

For Shame

I know why they say
they don't know
or why they don't name it
but like to shame it
because that would mean
we would have to then become it
and when we become that thing
that no one wants
you to be
the thing no one wants
you to see
the thing they don't want
you to see in you
it's better to look away
and just not say it
but to forget it
where it was
you were meant
to forget it
beneath the buried
photos and letters
passed down to you
amongst the shit
you penned in and over
there languishing
just beneath
the surface
on a coffee table
in a photo album.

Blindsided

Not knowing where you stand
in the memory
or where the memory lands
What was behind the shadows
now revealed
the conscious mind
meets the unconscious
to unravel a story
that seemingly
chokes you
and yet lulls you
back to sleep
A peak into
a window
that had been boarded up
where the light
shines in
on a truth
behind a lock
that was also being held down
by others
or thwarted —
a deviation
to throw me off track
but in the end
the truth
boomerangs back.

I Used To Look Away

I used to look away like I had to yesterday
as I was taught when I wasn't heard
by those who were meant to hear me
I used to look away and play along
like child's play when I wasn't seen
by those who were meant to see me
I used to look away and think the monster
would just go away if I looked away
but the problems would copulate and penetrate
and conceive and then birth
more echoes of black holes
So I learned to look the monster
right in the face to tell it what I needed
and slowly watch it dissolve as problems
were solved and tended to
and even mended too
Now there's a ring
of hope that rings true
there in the burn
where life now blooms
even when the
vines try to take up room
I rise above it all — like I wished
in my childhood bedroom
in full plume.

Recreate to Shed Dead Weight

Some people want to keep you
down
when you have   risen
and remind you
of who you were
in pain
as if to say
"survival" was you
but this thriving
you're doing
is allowed to shed
dead weight
like them —
to live anew —
in all that you do.

My Loyalty

What is loyalty?
Is it for you? or
Is it for me?
Should I be loyal
to someone
who has never
shown loyalty to me?
It's strange to think
that opinions are treated
like royalty
by our society
But when I appoint
myself a silver crown
or my own crimson gown
that others sit and frown
and act like clowns
when they think
I owe anyone
and everyone
— my loyalty
As though it's printable
like currency
as though it's permissible
to betray me
That's why it's liberating
to break free from
being loyal to others
to be loyal to yourself

It's not selfish
to treat yourself
like a royal
rather than
serving everyone
else first.

Into The Woods

Into the woods
Out of the weeds
-*And into my heart*

Hurt So Good

When hurt met love
and love met hurt
it hurt so good.
But love shouldn't hurt they say.
(Well, it was too late for me anyways.)
Because love had
always hurt
like the time
he hurt me
for hurting myself
and it hurt more
than hurting myself
(if that makes any sense).
I know it does
to those who know
what it's like to be spoon-fed
sweet poison
disguised as a gift.
And you drink it down
like a good girl
even when it makes you sick
because you've been conditioned
to just — go with it
to pander to every whim
to be amiable for them.
Well, I'm a bad girl now
I'm done listening to others
telling me what to do.
The hurt doesn't hurt so good, no more.

Super Moon

I saw the super moon light up over the Harbourfront
and over my life
when the mistress of darkness became the light
How is that for a slice of life?
The sun always gets the glory
but I want to know the moon's story?
How she remains so beautiful in the dark
How she remains loyal to the sun
even when he circles the earth
How she holds her own
and knows where she will be found
and when it's her time to shine
because she's in touch with her sacred divine
in life's design
weaving webs of happiness with heartbreak
How come no one ever said
it would be this way?
I saw the full moon today
It shone over the harbour and over my life.

Flickering Lights

I didn't just see the Vegas bling
where lights, camera, action are the thing
that makes the American dream
or makes them dream of the dream
because I had a dream
wasn't just a dream
No, really, it was spoken
and although we are broken
we can be repaired
like the shards of broken glass
that the Safed mystics
fuse together
It just has to be you see
living the dream
just being
It happened when I saw fireworks
for my first time
and probably the only time
and so it would have been the last time...
when I saw fireworks
from atop of the clouds
on a jet plane
So surreal it was a dream
and when I came home
I was so serene
when a firefly circled
my night sky
just you and I
right there by our side

on the other side of the window
is where the green light cracked
glided and flickered
green flecks of dreamy deep dreams...

Fluorescent Lights

I painted my nails a fluorescent pink
and my toes a fluorescent peach
because no one else is doing it
and it makes me happy.
Like the time I wore lime green to prom
that was when fluorescent strobe lights
and rave clothes were brightly dipped like fun dip
to make me as happy as a kid in a candy store.
(I know it's so cliche.
Well, I've learned to let it go.
It's not literary — I know.)
Remember when life was dipped
in bright fluorescent lights?
I don't care to stockpile the stockpiles
or add junk to the junkyard
I don't care to hoard with the hoarders
or add mines to the landmines.
I want to want the unwanted
the hidden gems in the lost and found
the misfits
they are my perfect fit —
the black lace fingerless gloves
that make the outfit.
I like to wear them because no one else wears them.
Remember when life was dipped
in the bright fluorescent lights?
in the bright lights?

When Life Is A Soup

I was swimming in soup
this was no alphabet soup
or zoodles
but more like doodles
on a pool noodle
holding on for dear life
on a raft
that has no mat or tact.
I wanted someone to build me a raft
until it was me who had to catch my breath
like *Life of Pi* on the raft
full of faith and reasons
and the present and the past
when you can sink or swim
— *You better run fast.*

Blood Orange Heart

She's so tired,
tired of being a temptress
tired of playing,
playing with the slings and arrows
of outrageous fortune

That pierce her pierced soul
draining her heart like the sweet juices
of a blood orange
in a serial killer's hands
Until there's nothing
but dried fruit
because her heart
is of no more use
just a fragmented fragment
of what it used to be
as she slips on an orange peel
before locking it in the glory box
Oh, it didn't have to be this way, she laments
as she eats the blood orange
by the light of the full moon in full bloom.

Blood Moon Heart

This is no blood orange heart
that lives in fear and abandonment
but a super blood moon
that inspires shadows to dance with the wolves
where transformations transpire
like rubbing sticks to make fire
There is no stopping the cycle
that spins through life, death, and rebirth
and there may just be that
moment where it all lines up
and the maiden, mother, and sage
merge to see the same perspective
Lifting the goddess to walk through the fire
bopping to her heart's desire.

Chasing Demons

These days I'm not chasing dreams
or dream catchers
but chasing demons
like a wedge of lime after a warm
shot of tequila
I'm not daydreaming either
lost in pink clouds of candy floss
being fed magical grapes
fairytales or sweet little lies
No, I'm turning over the soil
seeing all that has spoiled
all that has been sown
all that has grown
And how much more could fly
if I could just
chase those demons away
So I haunt them
in my life and in my dreams
chase them back into the corners
they cornered me into
With my back up against the wall
you thought I was going to fall
but that is when I glide
to levitate
when my heart balloons
over the full moon.

Swallowed Words Like A Baby Swallow

Her words begged for an answer
to the question but her pleading
eyes and desperate arms craved ignorance
I fawned, after all when that look
unfolded, unfounded in a smile
as the weight of the words
disappeared, vanished
like my voice swallowed into the
pit of my stomach like a baby swallow
devoured in a black-spotted memory
by a Doberman that set in
on watch, as her hug
held me tightly
it was all so delightfully
painfully neat...
...until the truth damn near
almost fell out of me...
and then slept with that enemy for
what must have been an eternity
inside of me dormant like a virus.

The First Winter Owl

The first winter we moved
into Anishinaabeg territory
we had no family to greet us
no friendly faces to meet us
except for that one winter owl
whose "hooo hooos"
ECHOED in the deep
of the Bear Creek woodlands
on a blue frozen night
serenading us from its perch
on the tree, of the tree that used to be

Because this winter
was empty quiet
when our winter owl
did not return
I guess he learned
to sojourn beyond the horizon
that careens the blue mountains
I will never forget the first winter owl.

Bluebells

He called me his bluebell
that afternoon in the parkette
and while bluebells are symbolic
of humility and gratitude
they also represent
everlasting love and constancy.
And in a world
where everything has been
topsy turvy
or hurly-burly
I clutch the bluebell so tightly
that my hands turn red.
Because to plant a new garden
you need to dig up the dead weeds
to see the forest for the trees.

Are You Sure?

Are you sure they ask?
Are you sure he said that?
Are you sure he did that?
Are you sure he meant that?
Are you sure you heard that?
Are you sure you saw that?
Are you sure you felt that?
Are you sure?
Yes, I am sure
as the day I was born
that your questions say more
about you
than they do me.

In the Pure and Bloody Waters

In the pure and bloody waters...
Is the water pure
or is it bloody?
Is it bloody pure
or pure bloody?
Sometimes you can't see
until you're in the thick of it
submerged head in the holy waters
of a full moon night
on a kayak in the Jordan river,
like a ritual bath
there in the pool of blood
is the truth
of those who bled into the ache
or washed the hurt and pain away
with a paintbrush painting
different strokes
to awaken what was once sleeping
as though set adrift.
I will wear this warm white wool cloak
wrapped around my heart and
the hearts entrusted to me
with hands that touch growth
peace and clarity;
home, heart, and humanity:
no matter how pure or bloody
the waters may be.

Makeup Heals

I'm so sick of hearing about the bad things that
makeup does to us
What about the good things it does for us?
Like when your face hurts so hard from the
depression
with puffy eyes from all those tearing tears
that the makeup soothes with rounded brush strokes
rounding all the hard edges
staining the skin in different hues

What about that?
Like when the makeup brings colour into darkness
with a new splash of nails at the nursing home
or that first time you pressed your lips
against the bud of a new tube of lipstick
after almost forgetting what lipstick even smelled
like when your nude lips were tucked
under a manmade mask for so long...

Black Swan Song

There's a black frozen
swan somewhere in
the depths of an Ontario
ice pond, forlorn but still
with a black swan song
at the base with feathers
covering her face
forsworn to starry
silent nights
her heart
like an icicle for so long.
Dripping from the
deep freeze or
the polar vortex
until a thaw
moves in
and the
icicle
begins to melt like a snowflake
on her long black eyelash.
Only to get caught back
in the snow belt before resuming
the ever looming
disappearance
of the
i
c
i
c
l
e.

Hope, Are You There?

Hope hasn't lived here
in a while, but now
I see her crooked smile
as she defrosts our hearts
in the most brokenness of parts

Hope hadn't lived here anymore
she hadn't walked through our door
but she seems to be staying
around this time and for a while
in a few lumps of unfolded piles

Hope is there, she's here
she's near, she's dear
she's around the corner
soon, she will appear

Maybe we can take her
on a little ride
by our side:
Hope, dear?
Are you, there?
Can you hear me?
Can anyone hear me?
Do we have a connection?
Is your mic on?

You're breaking up.
Is your video on?
It's fuzzy.
Hello?
Hope...
Can anyone hear me?

Oh, okay good...
It's working.
We have a connection now.
Hi, Hope.
How are you?
I was hoping we could work together

Maybe do a collaboration
~I Have High Hopes for us.

Bounce and Flow Are Gifted

When a weight is lifted
and bounce and flow are gifted
so we feel it —

Do they also see it?

What are we feeling?
(Isn't it fascinating?)
Now that we're feeling
our feelings relate
that can elate or deflate

By the time it gets to the place
where we make a date
take them out
to show them off
like taking our skeletons
on a night on the town

that is when we
step over
the feelings
and the weight
that was hovering
over us is lifted
and bounce and flow are gifted.

The Dead Sea Heals All Wounds

The dead sea heals
as it seeps into
wounds
you didn't even
know you had
and seals the old
only to refresh
and awaken
the new
like smelling sea salts

giving your body
back to you
floating atop
the sea of the dead
clad in clay
cleansing and washing away
every single bad day

because today is radiant
as the Mediterranean
sun shimmers
across the saltwater
purifying you.

I Played Dead

Who are we kidding
all those times I tried to run
away and hide from you
I only ended up running
away from myself.

Into such dark forests
you would have been shocked
to see me inside the place
where day turns into one night
of broken glass
propelling me to run
into the arms of the wrong lovers
hidden in between cannabis tokes
or some sexist jokes
dancing all night to numb the pain
not even knowing my own name.

I dulled my spirits
abandoned and then murdered them
until I was a paint splatter
of discarded roadkill
but I would have decomposed
like that recurring dream.

I never knew what that meant
But now I do
I was looking up
to save me from you.

But no one even knew
I had to be saved
or how badly I should
have been saved from the likes of you.

I couldn't escape
because who had I even become
when you parked yourself in there
poisoned all the fertility
until I had the courage
to stop playing dead
and lifted my head to be fed
by my own hand
to see that you were the one
who was dead
and I collided with myself
there again.

After running
hiding
splitting
doubling
shapeshifting
fawning
and shrinking...

I collided with myself
headfirst
and now —
I can't let myself go
I won't because
I will it
I am it —

I will never
let myself go,
again.

Shadows of the Willow

The sparrows chirp
what the sparrows know
the tiny sparrows of my sorrow
that flutter and flatter
the hollow shadows of the Willow tree
that now lives inside of me

They're the only ones
who have heard and seen
the tiny sparrows of my sorrow
that no one else knows

Where all the pain is set and primed
and lives and goes and then grows
into the hollow shadows of the Willow.

Lost in Rolling Meadows

Let's stroll through the rolling meadows
and taste the bittersweet-scented
dandelions crushed and stained
on the caps of our banged-up knees
like a whiff of honey beeswax
and soft blades of deep green grass.

Impressed with impressions
of petals in a book with a free spirit
that sprints like one of the Ingalls' girls
tumbling down into a free-falling fall
from innocence down the rolling meadows
of Kansas, reminding me of days spent like Grace
rolling down the hill before the red tent enveloped
me in company that smelled like mint tea
steeping in the land of white milk and golden honey
both blistery cool and warmly sweet.
When suddenly, I was ousted from the flower girl
stage and I didn't know that when I turned the page
I would be walking and then running into
the other side of where we lost ourselves
inside those rolling meadows of scattered white
wood anemone wildflowers stained in deep shades of
red.

The

humid

rain is so

peaceful as

it settles into
the earth, and the
birds' chirp, *for what
it's worth.* The humid rain
is so peaceful, it reminds me
of when you and I were in a hot
tent, with the flaps open, soaking
in the sun, earth, morning dew, against
me and also you...*(What was I supposed to
do, again?)* Oh right, just lay here — and *dig
into* me and you, *nothing else to do,* except for
listening to the tune of the *pit-pat, pit
pattering* rain, rippling, vibrating,
dripping into a pool of sweaty
afterglow. When the sun
comes out to greet the
moon, you know,
maybe that's the
time you suddenly
have to go. Since
you can't let
those moving
clouds, go as they
pierce the night sky,
and my hair frizzes
in wet locks of
curls, tangled
in summer's heat and

radiance humming
to nature, entangled in your
hands like rain
d
r
o
p
s

Your Body Is Poetry

There's nothing
like a body
that has been lived in
as in worn to the core
or built life within

A body is a house
in this house, I have lived
in this house, there has lived
life on the inside

That I wrote out and house
in stanzas with tangos and twists
and mango hurricanes
and many turns

A body is a house
in this house, I have lived
in this house, there has lived
life on the inside

But where there are tough falls
and waterfalls
battle scars
or a cross-stitch
or a faded stretch mark
a newly sprouted wrinkle
or a pox of a spot
there is also a beauty mark
or a lotus tattooed
landmark
scratched and etched out of
landmines

and memorized useless
landlines
with sun-flowered
landscapes
of vanilla dip, creamed skin
dripping in
life
lived.

Words Become Me

Words become me
thoughts become words
words fall all over me
like ink spills on a page
to soothe my brain
bring sunshine when there's rain
or rages down in pain at dawn
to sing the siren song
that hums me back to what I long for
those words transform me
and then transcend me
to another time and place
where I'm pressed up
against your face
or back in time, without a trace
tracing back to a *"me"*
that is no longer
so, in a word —
Words escape me
words beckon me
words soothe me
words haunt me
but most of all
-words become me.

I Waited For You

I waited for you
to meet me where it was
we first met

I retraced my steps
even the ones I leaped
stumbled, fumbled
and hopped over

As I rode the overpass
past the slippery
steep jagged rocks
and looked toward the clearing

Even when the nocturnal
wave was nearing
I still waited
for the dawn of healing
that I could hear
even when it never
seemed to hear me

So I waited and waited and waited

But then the waiting turned to such hating
and became a fearing of the morning cock crowing
spurned by all the mourning I'd been doing

All that time wasted *in waiting*
for others to show up
when they could never
even find themselves
— *let alone me*

And so it's time to descend
to wait for no end but those who ascend
to meet me in the plush, lush, hush
of intimacy, there in the place of
expectations — *(the ones that my mother*
told me to wish away) I take back my right to them
today.

The Ocean Awakens Me

It's been noisy in here
racing thoughts
and conflicting information
being dropped
everything is always piping hot
like holding a hot rock
or melting your tongue on a pop rock.

I don't know anymore
all I know is that when I find
a rhythm or a rhyme
or a piece of peace
the racing thoughts
fall at my feet
maybe I can finally outpace them
by slowing down.

That's right
in escaping the noise
I find peace in the raucous
in the fierce ocean waves
the anonymity and belonging of the crowd.
It's funny how I chose to search in places
louder than home
and yet rediscovered the ocean waves
caressing my soul
awakening me
to a sense of quiet
I hadn't quite touched before.

There is a Royal Moroccan: she lives inside of me

I am like royal Moroccan mint tea
it lives inside of me
royal like royalty

Did you know that Soberano means sovereign?

There is a Queen who lives inside of me

She made me believe even when they said
to throw away the make-believe

So when a colleague gifted me the tea
she reminded me of
the royal mint
in me

Mint
like the tea
bitter but yet sweet
when we add milk and honey

But no matter
I will guard me in high esteem
like a preserved tea leaf

There is a Royal Moroccan: she lives inside of me

The Day There Was No More Poetry

Would you believe me if I told you
that there was a time when
there was no more poetry?

I know it's so hard to believe
but my words wouldn't let me speak
I tied them up in tangled love notes
and knots of stifling forget-me-nots
because the pain was too great inside

But at first, I discovered words of poetry
in the corners of my teenage wasteland
scribbling and doodling in journals
that I haphazardly packed on overseas travels
once I settled into a suburban life that day
some sort of bizarre hypothermia emerged

For years I did not write, as the words
just didn't have much flight
when my womanhood endured arduous hikes
through the uneven planes of fertility
but sometimes a poem was shed
as it seeped through the cracks
and found the light of a new day

Then the words came floating on up
like an overflowing paper cup
with an echo of daylight falling on
the fresh orange, orgasmic
sunlight that would drape
the warehouse windows
of an underground rave

by the waterfront
at the break of a hot summer day
with reckless abandon
heating our cheeks
and paving every step of the way

I tell you
sometimes I still tread that fine line
but it is there on the fearless coastline
where I found the damp, cold
and tattered journals deep within ...

They say to move to the rhythm of your own body

but sometimes I gave a big finale when I should
have been standing still
and then I raved all night
and even took a little pill.

They say to move to the rhythm of your own body
But sometimes I froze and turned it all off
I didn't know I could say no or change my mind.
They say to move to the rhythm of your own body
But sometimes I pushed myself when I should have
been resting, kept testing and testing, it was a blessing
when I was forced to quit.

They say to move to the rhythm of your own body
But some hijacked it and treated it the way they
pleased— damn reckless, like a disease.
They say to move to the rhythm of your own body
Then my body deserted me
when the babies didn't implant —
again, again and yet, again and then even again.

They say to move to the rhythm of your own body
Still, I think it's finally time
I listened to my body with my mind...
I've been dragging around
this shell for so long that
I think it's time I show her
why I should hang on...
I can hear myself now.
I can heal myself now.
I can allow myself to move
to the rhythm of my own body.

Side Swept

Have you ever been side-swept?
(*so fast*) you didn't even
know what happened
but you were already rolling with it —
letting it roll all over you …

(*Side-swept*)

But then when you refocus
to make out the shadows in the closet
that dangled before you
dancing, prancing and laughing

Then what do you do?

The next time you're side-swept …
Do you sweep it all up before it erupts?

Or do you interrupt and call it out to face it?

I used to let it seep through the draft
as I practiced the art of sweeping it under the rug
(*that was when we weren't untying the knots*)

When you're side-swept it hits like *whiplash*
But now I walk through the freeze and face the fear

If you side sweep me —
You will be cleaning up that mess.
Side-swept.
It leaves you *verklempt*

There Are Words You Can't Take Back

There are words
there are words you
there are words you can't
there are words you can't take
there are words you can't take back
there are words that break
there are words —words there are.

But there are words
I can recognize
as part of your tape recorder
that playback
unraveling reel to reel
bunching up
twisting and turning
until it comes undone
and the cassette tape is useless.

I chucked out that Walkman
the one that used to come
prerecorded with all
of your words
that floated
around my head like headphones.

Instead, I walk
in a dead zone
of peace
from your words
and now when
they ping or ring
they don't quite sting
because I know

what they mean
and they're not meant for me.

There are words
there are words you
there are words you can't
there are words you can't take
there are words you can't take back
there are words that break
there are words —
words there

Let It Pass Through You

Have you ever noticed
when you call out
the dysfunction
that's mostly when
they want to quiet you
to quiet the dysfunction,
and so do you, *you really do.*

But that's why
you had to name it,
say it, and breathe it,
so you can
let it pass through you.

It touched you
and left an imprint
but it isn't you —
trauma healing is about
letting it move through you
and out of you.

This is mind-breaking
for those of us who ran
away to numb the pain
and ended up out of breath.

Then we named the dysfunction,
and they need to make you
become it, so you walk away,
as it passes through you,
and you leave it there at their feet.

Those Eyes

They say the eyes are the window to the soul
and I've come to believe it, *you know* —
so much that I can't let those eyes go.

Those eyes that smile, squint, or twinkle
in wonderment, perplexity, or reflection
the window that also reflects swirling darkness.

You can see it you know?
What it is that they just can't let go...

The most devastating eyes are the dead eyes
on some women who have sold their souls
It haunts me — that look that I can't let go.

Then there are those crazy eyes, *you know*
(I only caught on to these recently)
Now that I see them and can detect that threat
I see a thread that ties their pain together
and the chase for that high that settles
the pain and makes it rain down in shame.

I just wish those eyes could share their pain
of what they've seen and how to be free
despite the lack of reprieve.

But those eyes can also be beautiful
those irises spinning like records of purple rain
healing that pain of what was said and what was left
unsaid
— *it's no wonder that Oedipus stabbed his eyes out.*

I've always read eyes, ever since I could read
and sometimes it stung when their bleed
bled into me, and then onto me...

Those eyes can be a disguise
those eyes
that sing every day for you.

Make your eyes sing every day to you
even when their eyes don't know how to.

A Rare Gem In Your Eyes

Those eyes
untouched by life
open and sound
bright and optimistic
lush and vibrant
colours come together
like Baby Alive
taking it all in
veiled in such a thin line
a layer of protection
until life pierces the veil
rips it
tips it
twists it
spins it
brings it
then the Iris transforms
a new eye is born
tainted eyes dulled
memories evolved
what was seen
or unseen is found
blends and blooms
into a new moon
or monsoon

but when I see those eyes
in pictures
trapped in time
I can see again
life as a rare gem.

Even When I'm Careful

What's in a day?
and when a day takes such twists and turns
into the peaks and valleys of your life
that it feels like a year
How do you even begin to quell the fears?

When you're jarred
how do you fit it all back in the jar to place a lid on
it?
Even on a day when you were also popping
champagne bottles
Because no one else can see the untangled
entanglements
of the tapestry of my trauma, just as I was about to
rise...*again*

No one knows that April is already a hard month
(that's when I lost you
that's when I loved you
in our youth in Montreal)
No one knows that
for some reason trauma finds me here again

Where I meet myself victim and victor
silent and with roar, helpless and strong

Back in this space that they have made me belong
But this is not my song... or even my last song...

As words and actions
of perpetrators and enablers flood my brain
to land on my tongue, I now pick them apart...

Don't ask me if I'm sure
Don't question me because I questioned you.

Now I just have to figure out how to erase
those who crossed me
so carelessly that they feel nothing
while I'm left here feeling everything.

But I've worked so hard to tie up the loose ends
to display the tapestry of my trauma
that keeps unraveling
as it's threaded by new needles —

— *Even when I'm careful.*

I Was Silence

I

please don't feel bad
for not being able
to protect me
from a monster
         how were you to know?
that when she was supposed
to be watching me that he asked
         what I called my vagina
that when I repeated
the childhood pet-name
that had been passed down
(from the old country in Chernivtsi
a kosher Ashkenazi delicacy -a Knish)
that he would   prey on me
                    feed on me
silence me   scare me
              scar me
         how were you to know?
I felt suffocated when he breathed on me
like I was   disappearing
the way I did when I had to
         disassociate
maybe my kindergarten teacher was right
I needed my ears checked
or was it that everyone else needed their ears checked
when I said I didn't want to go there anymore when I said
I didn't want to …

II

...I hugged mom
when I came back home
saying "*I don't like it there*"
as she made dinner in the newly
renovated kitchen of denial
with her round belly
and applewood soft cheeks
-and simply thought
I was coming home
from babysitting
(how utterly and entirely—devastating)
and in that moment:

I was silence

when I knew mom wanted me to
not have a reason to cry
but the elder women all asked me *why*
(only the wrong elder got to me first)
she asked me not to tell anyone
I did it for her I told myself that night
before bed until the thought fell down
right out of my head
right there sitting up in bed
telling myself over and over and over
again how I was doing it for her

III

By the time the other elders had asked
I was preoccupied with the task of silence
and the silence loomed
for what felt like an eternity:
> *a lifetime had passed*
> *graduations earned*
> *marriages vowed*
> *homes settled*
> *kids and kids and more kids*
until the silence was lifted
a few months after she passed
repressed memories flooded back
like a heat wave from that summer
alone in the desert
carrying the just desserts
of what I inherited

I tell my story now for all the children
who can't find the words
to tell you the way
you would ask them to
so listen carefully
and guard them
from those closest
but know you are not to blame
and no matter how much darkness
touches you
monsters can never
dim your glow
(I Was Silence).

Let My Hurt Go

It's like the hurt was mine
all of theirs
their responsibility
is that why so many looked away
and crossed their fingers?

She saw it in me
she knew I had been hurt
like a scraped deer in headlights
but she washed me off in the bath

Was I carrying their secret?

Fuck you, this is my hurt
and I don't have to think of your hurt
when I decide to let go of mine.

And no I don't know
why my mind only
told me now
maybe it's because
the matriarchs
are no longer living
and I can spare one
from the hurt
of not knowing.

While the other
stuffed it down
so deep down inside of me
where no one but her
reached for me
and then it fell out of me
until I reached back in
and looked at the monster
right in the face.

Get Our Hands Dirty

I used to think
we could wait it out
that one day
we would outrun it
outsmart it
and finally, make it

But there is no waiting
only enduring
and making time to rejoice

Without it ever
being the right time
because when the highs
are so high
and the lows
are so low

We can't wait
for the moment
to spoil
after laying down
all that soil.

We Must Find Our Worth To Lift This Curse

It's not a dream-not even make believe
It's also not a sob story to make you think
I don't care what this says to you

All I know is that the only thing left to do
is to tell you what I saw
what I see in the women
around me and how this came to be

I've watched many strong, beautiful women
have their hearts locked up in a cage
and the women not even knowing
it was their heart to begin with

This is the fairy tale I never dreamed
was never really shown to me
it was always some old woman
stealing her jewels and the prince
was oh so charming

But in real life, well, real life
he's dressed as an old woman
hoarding her light
with everything in sight
raping her of her delights and life
filling himself with it
then emptying her
draining her
her earth
her lifeforce
in my environment, around me
inside of me in families, in societies

My women, we must find our worth
to lift this curse
that no one knows about
who isn't behind our
closed doors.

Butterfly Lady

I'm
getting better
at giving myself permission
to relax and do nothing

To do something but nothing. Nothing
but something. I wasn't always
like this. Maybe it was the
Covid cocoon I had to
build around me
but suddenly
the fortress

is uneasy, sometimes
queasy on this quest into
the unearthed, unknown, untrodden,
untouched Wilderness of the Ontario
backcountry that becomes me when I'm back home
to learn

how to fly like a fluttering,
opening, butterfly
taking up space
coming there like a lady
in the green shimmering summer sky
dancing with the floating,
shattering northern
lights
once more.

Black Crow

I saw a black crow today
perched atop a tree
(she says she talks to angels they say)
somehow it was both the owner and the owned
as it strutted like a peacock

It reminded me of the peace
that enveloped me
last summer when a
fluttering hummingbird welcomed me

Is the crow greeting me?
Is it retreating or leading?
A good sign, or a bad sign?
Is it wisdom, or a warning?

Does it even ever matter
when the darkness is here to stay
the black crow knows that
-and flies above the cracked green
Northern lights, *anyways...*

The True North

We either creep
at a snail's pace
or fly like a bird

but sometimes
the distance between
cutting corners
and turning corners
becomes reality meeting
realized dreams
forming a sacred dance

because we haven't
really lived until
we've trekked
no man's land
or is it the badlands
or better yet the highlands
no, no that's not it
(that's not it at all)
it must be the backcountry
(after all)
in the arms of the Arctic
down to the tip and dip
of the Blue Mountains

Yes, like a true Canadian
—*the true north strong and free*

It's time we've found
that the road less traveled
is where we want to be

Here and there, like a true Canadian
—*the true north strong and free*

Is where we flutter and glide peacefully.

Glimmers

They say
you can turn triggers into glimmers
They say
you can pull the trigger or see the glitter
They say
you can turn that frown upside down
They say
you can pull yourself out of the dark
I say
I've been facing my triggers
only after digging out of the whirlwind
of disasters that formed into plaster
swirls on the ceilings of my heart and home
I say
I've been unearthing the triggers
suddenly, they aren't that much bigger
and I can step outside of me to see
Glimmers
reflect back at me
vibrating and humming like the
shimmering northern nights.

Seeing Blue Jay

Sometimes you just need to see
something unexpected
to see life anew again
like seeing a blue jay
minding its own business
fluttering and strutting
around the school courtyard
enrobed in blue and white
and a crown of spiked
or slicked-back heights
to remind you of childhood
when life was more in sync
and in tune with nature
and the self
and things like
heaven and with hell
(these days there's no way to tell)

Before the dreaded bell
made everything smell
like trouble brewing so exponentially
that even *the centre cannot hold*
so that the blue jay leads me down a path
towards my way back to innocence
because living jaded jade
is like living in the shade
and I want to live
in colour *again*
as vibrant as the blue crest
of a blue jay.

Breaking Up With the Cobalt Blues

the blue is insidious now —
cold and bold
cobalt blue
hard and prominent —
the stain of man
hope flickering
like the warmth of the fire
the monster saw
or the green light
that mesmerized Jay Gatsby
hard and soft, calm and strong
scrolling across a TV screen
in a hauntingly familiar
yet forgotten
hypnotizing
fuzzy blizzard
but the truth is...

...I prefer ocean blue
turquoise or sepia
with a romantic flair and flavours
to indulge in
when life is so harsh and hazy
when the deep is so blue —
it makes me want to
break up with the torrid waves of
-the cobalt blues...

Stay Gold

Dedicated to Ms. Pitcairn

Stay gold—*stay true*
 it used to just be the important
thing to do in our youth
—*to seek justice and truth.*

Even when living in broken homes,
or hanging on the wrong side of the tracks,
you still had real friends
but when life eats away at memories
and the golden sheen has dulled,
or you had mistaken gold-plated jewels
for the real thing, only then do you see
that perhaps when the good die young
that is the only way to *stay gold*
and suddenly *staying gold*
 means so much more than it used to
now that you know what it is to rust.

You, my friend, are forever golden and full of trust.

The Afterword

Finding Rest in the Unrest of a Friend's Suicide

That was his choice. I had to learn to hold and honor it, instead of judging and condemning it. That was the only way for me to honor his memory and the love that we once shared.

It was a Saturday morning at the end of April 2017 when I learned of the news. I had been making the kids breakfast; it was chocolate chip pancakes that day. The pancakes had tears in them as the kids witnessed the news hit me like a ton of bricks. I had to grasp that James Buchanan (1975-2017), my boyfriend during undergraduate studies was gone. He had committed suicide as he had endured too much pain during his ongoing battle with depression. Besides the shock of the loss, I was struck with guilt over not having been able to help him. This was because I had a premonition earlier that week to which I hadn't listened. At the time, I had been telling myself that had I acted on that instinct, I could have made a difference.

Now that time has passed I recognize that nothing I could have said or done would have made a difference. That was his choice. I had to learn to hold and honor it, instead of judging and condemn it. That was the only way for me to honor his memory and the love we once shared.

Initial Feelings of Guilt and Blame

That week before I heard the news of James's suicide, I found myself watching 13 Reasons Why, a Netflix series on a woman's suicide. I never finished the series because I learned of his suicide when I was in the middle of the series and I could not bear to watch it again.

But as I was watching one episode a sudden realization hit me: the battle with suicide never leaves, instead it's a disease that sits with the individual like a life sentence.

As my mind, body, and soul took in this realization, my thoughts wandered to my dear friend James. I had just always assumed that his battle was in the past and that that was then, but I was sorely wrong. I actually did not know much about James's mental health or past struggles with suicide because he shielded me from a lot of it when we were together. When he finally informed me of his suicide attempt that occurred a few months after we began to date, he told me that he had moved on and taken care of it; he had sought help and that it was in his past now. I had no reason not to believe him. Maybe he also had no reason not to believe himself.

Except when I had this realization at the start of the same week that he would later commit suicide, something inside of me told me to reach out to him. But being the mom of three boys ages 1, 3, and 7 at that time, I didn't have the bandwidth to listen to that internal voice, and I did not reach out to say hi. Actually, while we had stayed connected over the last 15 years, the few years before his death we had fallen into peaceful silence. We were busy with our respective lives. The last time we had a meaningful exchange was May 2015 when he commented on a picture of me, saying I still looked the same as he had remembered me.

Due to not listening to my instincts, and the trauma I was facing, the first emotions I felt were that I failed him. I thought that I could have done something even through cyberspace. I somehow knew in some deep, intuitive, untaped space that rose to the surface a few days before his suicide that something just wasn't right, but I hadn't acted on that feeling.

Writing as Therapy in Accepting the Suicide of a Friend

I also was unable to find closure because I couldn't attend the funeral. At the time, as the mom of a young family, I didn't have the time, means, and space to ingest the trauma. I did turn to write as therapy, however. The initial drafts were all very raw and full of anger for what had happened.

Then at the time, I discovered a poem that James had written a few years ago that he chose to share with me entitled, "A Perfect Moment." I shared it with his family in an email and they shared it as the service as part of his eulogy.

I was forever grateful to be able to contribute something to that day. I was grateful that while we were two very different people and my love of poetry inspired him and that he felt comfortable enough many years later to share it with me in one of our online chats.

His poem is what helped heal my heart. Both in the writing, I cherished from him, and the writing I was beginning to do surrounding his suicide.

Through writing, I was able to work through the feelings of guilt, blame, and anger to find some acceptance and peace. But first I had to work through all of the preconceived notions that surround suicide that society fed us for so long.

Unlearning Suicide Stigma to Learn Compassion

I had to unlearn all of the things I learned about suicide. The most popular misconception of suicide is that it is a selfish act; this type of thinking hurts and does nothing to honor their memory, spirit, or inner struggle.

James definitely wasn't selfish either. He was very giving. In fact, he helped make my dreams come true. Even after we had gone our separate ways, as a flight attendant, he granted me one of his friends and family plane tickets which I used to backpack across Europe in 2001.

Next, I had to face the stigma of suicide being defined as cowardly. I had to unlearn that only cowards commit suicide because James was no coward.

James was brave. He was a sociology major with a heart of gold. He had done a study where he posed as a homeless man to challenge stigma and raise awareness. He was so excited to grow and learn. I will never forget running into him on the streets of Montreal posing as a panhandler.

In learning how to heal I had to learn not to use reason or logic to understand his decision to commit suicide. I had to use my heart. I had to dig deep to find compassion. I had to carve out space for him to honor his choice and memory.

In doing so I was able to find some sense of peace and reconciliation. I also had to heal some regret surrounding having not stayed connected the last few years before his death.

Then I had to be compassionate as I was engrossed in growing my family and I got lost in it. But just because I faced my inner demons and preconceived notions, does not mean others did.

Unfortunately, in speaking about James's suicide sometimes I have to face these outdated notions surrounding mental health and suicide.

Sometimes I have to hear these feelings echoed in others but rather than let it get to me, I choose to interrupt this dialogue. I choose to push back against outdated and punitive notions surrounding suicide.

Takeaways

Finding rest in the unrest that a friend's suicide leaves behind is an ongoing struggle but one that is made more possible by choosing compassion over shame.

In talking openly about suicide the stigma surrounding it can be challenged.

I understand that individuals all heal differently and that healing grief is never linear but I would like to think that in choosing compassion that this journey is less arduous.

We do not have to hold all the shame and stigma that society has fed us surrounding suicide.

We do not need to smear their lives and memories in outdated narratives.

Instead, we must raise awareness, compassion, and understanding to accept that this was their decision. This was how it was meant to be.

He Saved My Life, But He Died Young, And So I Pay It Forward:

The silver lining in the silver dress.

That spring night in 1995, Dylan Shulman(1977-2003) saved my life. He had no hesitation in caring for me. The unbelievable part, however, was that he did not regularly attend raves, but luckily, he did that night. Even though I thanked him for the night he saved my life, it was not enough. Even though I thanked him the next morning, it was not enough. Even though I thanked him again the next week, it was not enough. Even though I thanked him yet again when he served my family and me at Red Lobster, years later, it was not enough. No, it was never enough.

Because then I had to thank him by sharing my bittersweet story with his grief-stricken mother, Libby, who lost Dylan in a bicycling accident on May 27, 2003, at the young age of 25.

And so I also thanked him in his afterlife, sharing our story with his grieving mother.

I will never stop being grateful to Dylan. Since he saved my life when I was a teenager, and I got a second chance at life because of him, I consider my role as a teacher to be my way of paying it forward.

The Night Dylan Saved My Life

Where am I? I said as I slipped into an abyss of faceless voices that echoed as I struggled to stay with the high-bass speakers that shook my stunned body.

"You're at a rave," he said.

"A rave. What is a rave?" I managed to mumble.

"An all-night dance party. You're here with friends. You're going to be okay. I got you," he whispered into my ear.

And I believed him. He just kept on telling me that I was going to be okay, and so I believed him. What other choice did I have?

The next thing I knew someone was wiping the puke off my silver baby-tee dress that I had sown a silver moon badge on (I had bought the badge from Kensington market the week before). But I didn't really know who was caring for me, since I was so out of it, and my "friends" had abandoned me at the downtown Toronto rave.

I remember a girlfriend coming to take the whistle from around my neck ("ravers" liked accessories, such as a whistle, gloves, or glow-in-the-dark batons), so that she could use it since I was of no use. You don't forget moments like that. Even in my state of delirium, my body and mind awoke when she put her hands around my neck to selfishly take the lanyard.

Ecstasy was the raver's drug of choice, but as with any street drug it was unregulated. For the most part, my friends had been able to buy from "reliable" sources but I was excluded from the group drug deal that night, because an ex-boyfriend was involved and he wanted to "protect" me.
In other words, he wanted to control me.
Consequently, I went out on a limb to trust Steve who had just begun attending our local high school in the predominantly middle-class suburb of North York.

I Met The Devil in Disguise and My Guardian Angel

But that reckless loser, Steve, almost killed me. He damn well knew he was giving me some dirt-cheap street drug known as Phencyclidine PCP, instead of ecstasy but he wanted to turn a profit, so he didn't care what happened to me.

Though I bet he didn't think that was the night I would down an entire pill. I still remember when the drug deal went down on the dance floor. I should have known by the way he lurked that he was up to no good. When he came around 30 minutes later to "check" on me, I thought it was peculiar when he was alarmed that I took the whole capsule.

Though I was the victim of a drug deal gone wrong, and so I ran into bad luck due to a bad apple, and my own poor choices, little did I know that on the same night I would also meet my guardian angel. In fact, the person who ended up caring for me was not even one of my best friends. Dylan was more of an acquaintance since we had common friends. If Dylan hadn't been there that night, I don't think I would have made it.

It was him who ensured I drank water and didn't choke on my vomit.

Through the Eyes of A Mother

With every year that passes, I see my overdose experience in a different light. At first, I saw it as a teenager who was grateful for a second chance, and eventually related to it as a teacher who wanted to pay it forward.

But since becoming a mother, suddenly my vantage point has shifted. Now, I look at it through the eyes of a mother. That is why I was compelled to share my story with his mom: to celebrate the life that his life gave to me.

I don't talk much about my teenaged years. They were mostly positive, and while I didn't take school seriously, I was thankful to smarten up on time to go to university. But it was touch and go for a while there.

I lost myself in parts of my teenaged years, and would then find myself. It's a cycle that I would also come to know in my adult years, as I battled to find a balance between healing and running away from my internal demons.

But as a teenager, I often ran away from myself by seeking out the wrong friendships or relationships. Despite my penchant for being a people-pleaser, I still managed to also attract good people into my life like Dylan.
And that I will forever be grateful for.

Today, I Pay It Forward

As a high school teacher of over 15 years, I have met many teens, some of whom wanted to run away from themselves and jump out of their own skin. Some feel like they don't belong, others feel as if they are numb or plain old dumb.

Still, I focus on honing a growth mindset as opposed to a fixed mindset so that students know they can always improve because my students know that I believe that everyone is smart in their own way.

Some students don't have anyone at home to care for them the way they need to be cared for. As a teacher who taught in the public and private school system, I witnessed the tragedy of some students never having anyone to expect anything from them. I am telling you that generally speaking, the more underprivileged the student is, the more they respond positively to a caring adult. That is if they can stand to accept someone caring about them. At first, many of my students try to push me away but when I don't give up, eventually, they open up. Students tend to do well for me because I expect them to try their best, reward them for such, and hold them up to a higher standard. I also play off their strengths to foster confidence. Sometimes a student just has to know he or she has a fighting chance to even want to try to succeed.

When people hear that I teach teens they often wonder why I do it. I mainly do it because I am passionate about my subject and teens. Above all, I strive to foster self-identity, critical thinking, and interpersonal relationships built on trust, accountability, fairness, and respect.

For example, sometimes teenagers need to know that showing up to class late is better than not showing up at all. When they walk through my door they are welcomed, instead of being chastised for being late. I create a safe space for teens to grow, learn, question, and turn to—a space where respectful dialogue and conversation are fostered.

That is such a gift.

Takeaways

In a letter to his parents, Dylan expressed gratitude to his mother when he said, "She has taught me the finer things in life like true love and companionship for others and that is something I love about her." He certainly understood the importance of caring for others in the same selfless way he cared for me that night at a Toronto rave in 1995. It's that gift of life that he protected for me when I was full of reckless abandon that inspires me to pay it forward.
I pay it forward to thank Dylan for being my guardian angel.

It was because of him that I found a silver lining in the silver dress that came home full of puke and gum stuck to it. And the badge had been mysteriously ripped off.

It was because of that night that today I am inspired to give back and make someone else's world more positive.

Thank you, Dylan, for helping me to help others.

About the Author

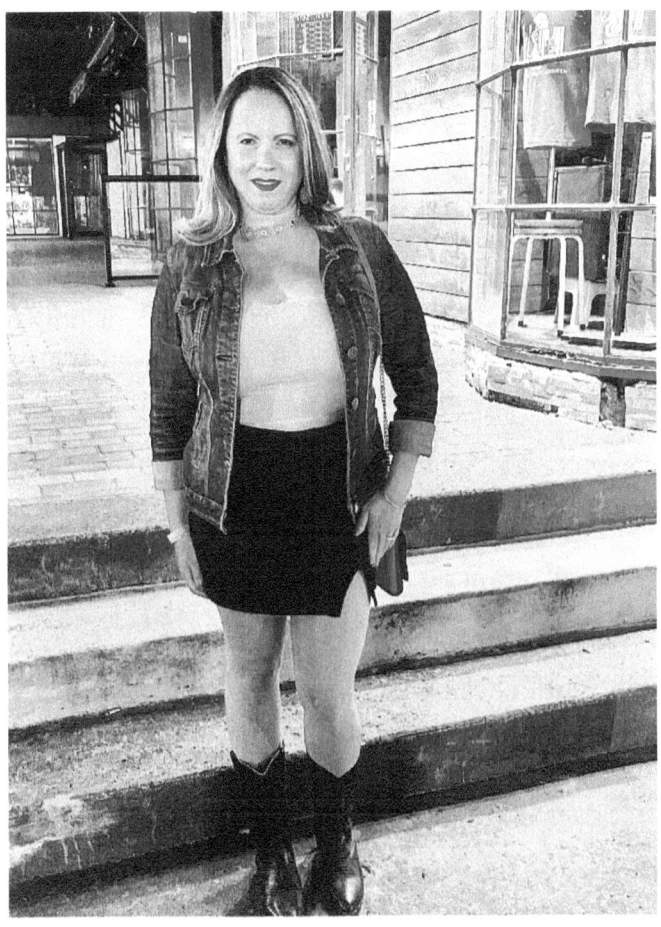

Lindsay Soberano Wilson is a mom, teacher, internationally published author, and creator of *Put It To Rest*, a mental health literary hub.

Her debut poetry collection *Hoods of Motherhood: A Collection of Poems* (Prolific Pulse Press, 2023) reflects on Soberano Wilson's portrayal of becoming a mother. Her poem, from this collection, "**The Japanese Red Maple**" was nominated for a Pushcart Prize, and her work was recently nominated for the Best of the Net.

Born in Toronto, Canada, Lindsay is the granddaughter of Spanish Moroccan immigrants and Romanian Holocaust survivors. Her chapbook *Casa de mi Corazon: A Travel Journal of Poetry and Memoir* (Poetica Publishing, 2021) explores how her sense of community, Canadian Jewish identity, and home was shaped by travel.

Lindsay graduated with an Honours Bachelor of Arts in Creative Writing and English from Concordia University and earned a Master of Arts degree in English and a Bachelor of Education from the University of Toronto.

Recent publications include *Jewish Women of Words, Fine Lines Literary Journal, Fevers of the Mind, Avalanches in Poetry III: Poetry, Writings & Art Inspired by Leonard Cohen, Spillwords Press, Cadence, Prolific Pulsations* and *Proof of Life* anthology in honour of 10-7.

In 2023, she earned a scholarship for teachers from the Canadian Society for Yad Vashem to The World Holocaust Remembrance Center in Israel. Lindsay is a member of the Feminist Caucus via The League of Canadian Poets where she and fellow poets amplify women's voices. She is writing a memoir about being a third-generation Holocaust survivor.

Review

Engraved Roses

In "Every Rose Has A Thorn" Lindsay Soberano Wilson remembers an engraved rose in a mirror above a mantle in her childhood home, and compares it to a rose that blooms, withers and dies. *Breaking Up with the Cobalt Blues* is about art and nature, and fragility and strength. The author processes the loss of a dear friend who has taken his own life. She places poems directly about that tragic loss in with others about her life before, during, and after a romantic relationship that began when they met as students in Montreal. Fittingly, poignantly her book begins with a lyric by her late friend, James Buchanan, that celebrates life. It is titled "The Perfect Moment." The trajectory of Soberano Wilson's book is located metaphorically in that mirror with its engraved rose: cracked by the shock of realization, shattered by despair, and put back together by a resilience of self. She speaks not only for and about herself, but for other women and for humankind.

    The mirror cracks, the rose withers. The rose in the mirror and the rose in the garden are one in the poet's emotional landscape. While art comes from joy, it also comes from pain. Her emotional trauma takes on the shape of poems. The mirror cracks, the thinking, feeling person weeps, grieves, rages inside, living with her loss. Her grief is conveyed in phrases such as "I howl but nothing comes out/ Screams I suffocated into my pillow/ a commotion of motions/ I go on as I was because I can't heal, and Suicide...there—I said it." Yet in the midst of this shock, the poet's trauma, there is perhaps a foreshadowing in "A Hummingbird Sang For Me Today."

> any minute now the joy is meant to sing
> and hum a new tune
> by tuning the untuned into the tuned
>
> it sang anew
> the hummingbird sang
> the hummingbird sang for me today
> the bearer of good news they say.

Yet she is shattered by despair, in the recent past of the Covid pandemic, "while babies are born in quarantine and the dead die alone." Her emotional isolation is compounded by social isolation. It is as if she talks to her muse when she says "release me of the woman they see/ when the landscape drifts...how do you find a fit?/no one is here...to give me what is left/ my heart burst open like shards of glass/ I want her to know I see her." It is as if she is outside herself, (emotionally she is), talking to and about herself. She says to and of her dear friend who has left this world "who you and I were...unlocks an I that is no more." In "I Tripped on a Wound Today" she notes:

> My intergenerational trauma wound is showing: it was exposed, punctured, and is gushing blood into puddles on the floor of my heart, and on the helm of my soul.

The story's title *Channeling my Inner Anne Frank* in a *Pandemic* followed by a correction from the   Twitter feed of the SS in Germany aka *The Globe and Mail* who said they were making a "clarification" — not an "apology" but a correction, that the story should read *Lessons in Living from Anne Frank*.

In her despair, she does not flinch but rather confronts the awful face of her trauma, which leads to a realization of history, and Anne Frank, who wanted desperately to live, and in her brief time on earth lived life to the fullest.

And near this wound poem in the book there is the poem "New Life," which is brief, and lovely, a precursor to the resilience that enables the poet to climb out of the deep dark hole she is in.

Only she can put herself back together. She does so with the realization that she is not alone. She notes the bravery and courage of Anne Frank, and the tribulations of all women, many of whom have been persecuted, oppressed, silenced because they were/ are women. And yet "the garden awaits the hands that held on to hope." In "Chasing Demons" she says, "I'm turning over the soil/ seeing all that has spoiled/ all that has been sown/ all that has grown." She turns over the soil with the strength of her hands and her spirit. Also with her voice. In "Silent Loud" there is the line "to curate artistry from pain," precisely what this poet has done.

Breaking Up With The Cobalt Blues is a sprawling book, as it must be. Many lines and passages are worth noting that have been excluded here. As one whole collection it is not an easy read but it is as rewarding as it is unsettling and consoling in its ultimate note: I love and am loved. Lindsay Soberano Wilson's voice is clear and passionate. The segments of our lives don't come in tidy little packages. Life is messy, life is miraculous. In her book art imitates life, reflects life, like a mirror. In one poem she says, "Feel me." She suggests breath fogging a mirror, the mirror with the engraved rose from childhood. Mirrors, crack, roses wither and die. The poems in this book were written by a thinking, feeling, caring woman. That much is clear.

Peter Mladinic, author of House Sitting, and The Homesick Mortician

www.ingramcontent.com/pod-product-compliance
Lightning Source LLC
Chambersburg PA
CBHW031511120626
46545CB00005B/1833